UNOFFICIAL CHAPLAIN

A Handbook for Everyday Service to the People Around You

by

Warren Crank

CHI BOOKS

CHI-Books,
PO Box 6462, Upper Mt Gravatt,
Brisbane, QLD 4122, Australia

www.chibooks.org
publisher@chibooks.org

Unofficial Chaplain – A Handbook for Everyday Service to the People Around You

Copyright © 2017 by Warren Crank

Print ISBN: 978-0-6480116-2-0

eBook ISBN: 978-0-6480116-3-7

Under International Copyright Law, all rights reserved. No part of this eBook may be reproduced, stored in a retrieval system, or transmitted in any form, including by any means electronic, mechanical, photocopying or otherwise in whole or in part without permission in writing from the publisher, except in the case of sermon preparation, reviews or articles and brief quotations embodied in critical articles. The use of occasional page copying for personal or group study is permitted and encouraged. Permission will be granted upon request.

Unless otherwise indicated, Scripture is taken from the HOLY BIBLE, NEW INTERNATIONAL VERSION®. NIV®. Copyright © 1973, 1978, 1984, 2011 by Biblica. Inc. Used by permission of Zondervan. All rights reserved.

Printed in Australia, United Kingdom and the United States of America.

Distributed in the USA and internationally by Ingram Book Group and Amazon.

Also available from: www.bookdepository.co.uk and other outlets like Koorong.com in Australia.

Distribution of eBook version: Amazon Kindle, Apple iBooks, Koorong.com and others like Barnes & Noble NOOK and KOBO.

Editorial assistance: Anne Hamilton

Cover design: Dave Stone

Layout: Jonathan Gould

DEDICATION

To military chaplains, past and present,
for their courageous faith on the frontline.

(Anzac Day Centenary, 2017)

CONTENTS

Foreword

Introduction		1
The Unofficial Chaplain's Prayer		4
CHAPTER ONE:	**C**ommissioned by God	5
CHAPTER TWO:	**H**olistic ministry	9
CHAPTER THREE:	**A**mbassador for Christ	13
CHAPTER FOUR:	**P**repared to share hope	17
CHAPTER FIVE:	**L**everage relationships for good	21
CHAPTER SIX:	**A**nticipate antagonism	25
CHAPTER SEVEN:	**I**ntercessory prayer	29
CHAPTER EIGHT:	**N**udge	33
CHAPTER NINE:	Flooding the zone	37
Postscript		39

Endnotes

About the Author

FOREWORD

In his book, the 'Unofficial Chaplain', Pastor Warren Crank shows us how we can more effectively help and reach the people around us. Our mission is to point people towards Jesus. The problem is that we're not always sure how to do this in ways that seem natural and respectful. This is where the idea of being an 'Unofficial Chaplain' comes in. Not many of us will be preachers but all of us can be Unofficial Chaplains. This book will show you that!

Chaplains continue to be respected. Their work in schools, with the armed forces and emergency services personnel is highly regarded. Chaplains are well known for the way that they care about people, whoever they are, whatever they've done. Warren has been a sports chaplain for many years and writes out of that experience. He has worked with the North Queensland Cowboys (NRL), Norths Devils (QRL) and, now, the Brisbane Broncos (NRL). I know, myself, of so many stories where official and unofficial Chaplains have touched lives in small and huge ways. Chaplains change lives as God points them in the right direction and they in turn point those around toward Christ. They present Christ in actions and words, lived out in relationship.

This book teaches eight Bible-based and field-tested chaplaincy attitudes and approaches. Each one will assist you greatly to help people and, to use Warren's words, nudge them towards Jesus at the same time. I believe that if more and more people embrace this chaplain lifestyle – at work, in their community, on university campuses, in the pub or on their sports team - we will see God do great things! What a privilege and how humbling it is to be called by Christ to show His love to those around us.

I encourage you to read this book and put what it says into practice. I know I will and I know it will make an amazing difference!

Jennifer Allen
Dean of Students for the University of Newcastle,
Unofficial Roadie for the Bob Corbett Band and the Mark Hotel.

INTRODUCTION

Chaplaincy: its history and living legacy

Christian chaplaincy has its origins in the life and service of St Martin of Tours (316-397). After Martin joined the Roman army, legend has it that he cut off half his cape to clothe a naked beggar. Sometime later, Christ appeared to him in a dream wearing the half-cape given to the beggar. Martin was baptized soon after and began to reach the people around him with love and the gospel of Christ. What remained of Martin's cape was preserved in a church which became known by the Latin name *cappella*. The term *capellanus*, from which we derive 'chaplain', was the title given to the priest whose special ministry it was to protect the cape.[1]

Later, the title 'Chaplain' was given to Christian ministers who once had charge of a chapel but were reassigned to special ministries *outside the church*. Charlemagne, a medieval emperor who ruled much of Western Europe, appointed chaplains to conduct religious ceremonies in the royal palace. These *cappella* served the monarch as advisers in matters both sacred and secular. The practice of kings appointing personal chaplains became widespread throughout western Christendom.[2] More recently, the title 'Chaplain' has been used for Christians serving God and people in a wide range of special ministries outside the church; including the armed forces, emergency services, schools, hospitals, prisons, sports clubs and embassies.[3]

Chaplaincy has widespread acceptance. The role is highly regarded. This reputation was forged on battlefields, like Gallipoli, as Christian clergy served military personnel under extreme duress and at great risk to their own lives.[4] For more than 100 years,

> The title 'Chaplain' was given to Christian ministers who were reassigned to special ministries outside the church.

Australian military chaplains have been there to listen to, support, encourage and pray for people in times of crisis. This good standing has been hard-earned and won. As Colonel C. J. Brewer said in a chaplains' conference opening address, "Even people who have no previous experience with chaplains will usually respond to their approach in a positive way."[5] To embrace the role of chaplain is to identify with a respected and noble tradition.

The Season for Unofficial Chaplaincy

As Cam Butler, head of Sports Chaplaincy Australia, says in his endorsement: people "don't want religion but they do want authentic chaplains. Someone brave enough and close enough to care." You can be an authentic chaplain without the title! You can be an Unofficial Chaplain. God has strategically positioned you to influence the world around you. You are probably located at or near the perceived centre of someone's existence. This is especially true of workplace contexts. Australian author, Roy Williams, wrote:

> More than two decades ago, the (now) veteran sociologist Hugh Mackay identified paid work as the new centre of an individual's existence in Australia. Subsequent events have confirmed Mackay's thesis in spades. For most men, and some women too, the workplace is the central social institution, the environment in which adults find their identity.[6]

I would say that this applies to senior sports teams as well. Serious sportspeople find their identity and sense of belonging wrapped up in their chosen sport and team. This would translate across many environments where people are passionate and committed; be they gardening clubs, community groups, cause-driven collectives, places of intellectual pursuit and such. If you are on the 'inside' in these contexts, then you are situated *like no other* to impact those colleagues and comrades. You are where you are because God loves those people and is reaching out to them, through you!

But how can you best help and influence people in ways that are natural and respectful? Perhaps you don't see yourself as an 'evangelist' or a 'preacher'. This is where the idea of becoming an Unofficial Chaplain comes in. Hundreds of people are discovering that the principles taught in this book help them to be much more intentional and effective in reaching the people around them. The number of Unofficial Chaplains is multiplying. You can join this growing missional movement. We'd love you to! This is the Season for Unofficial Chaplaincy.

I have been a chaplain for many years. My chaplaincy journey began with the 2008 Rugby League World Cup. Since then, I've been the official Chaplain of the North Queensland Cowboys National Rugby League team, the Norths Devils Queensland Rugby League team and I have recently been appointed as Chaplain for the Brisbane Broncos National Rugby League team. I'm a registered chaplain with Sports Chaplaincy Australia. Many of the ideas shared in this handbook have been learned from other chaplains and in the exercise of my own chaplaincy ministry. These ideas have been field-tested. I am convinced that the chaplaincy attitudes and approaches taught in the *Unofficial Chaplain* handbook are transferable. They will help you serve the people around you whatever the context—be it work, study or play. Adopting a chaplaincy mindset will increase your influence in a way that is spiritual, practical and credible. I want to encourage you to think of yourself as an Unofficial Chaplain, assigned to special ministry *outside the church*.

This handbook provides boot-camp-type orientation for new Unofficial Chaplains. It will also serve to remind those already engaged in this ministry of the essential fundamentals of effective chaplaincy.

THE UNOFFICIAL CHAPLAIN'S PRAYER

"Heavenly Father,

Today, I am commissioned to do good to the people around me.

If someone has a need I can meet, enable me to see it and meet it.

Help me be a credible ambassador for Christ, one who serves diligently and models integrity.

May I always be prepared to share my faith and hope in simple, appropriate ways.

Help my relationships deepen and my spiritual influence increase as I invest time in people.

Give me the strength to accept antagonism and to respond with a blessing.

Stir me, Holy Spirit, to pray for people privately and with them opportunely.

Today, Lord, help me nudge someone in your direction.

AMEN."

KEY BIBLE READING

"For, whoever would love life and see good days must keep their tongue from evil and their lips from deceitful speech. They must turn from evil and do good; they must seek peace and pursue it. For the eyes of the Lord are on the righteous and His ears are attentive to their prayer, but the face of the Lord is against those who do evil." Who is going to harm you if you are eager to do good? But even if you should suffer for what is right, you are blessed. "Do not fear their threats; do not be frightened." But in your hearts revere Christ as Lord. Always be prepared to give an answer to everyone who asks you to give the reason for the hope that you have. But do this with gentleness and respect, keeping a clear conscience, so that those who speak maliciously against your good behaviour in Christ may be ashamed of their slander" (1 Peter 3:10-16).

1

COMMISSIONED BY GOD

Chaplains who serve in the armed forces are generally commissioned officers. When a military chaplain commences ministry, there is a special commissioning service. This ceremony is a public validation of the chaplain's role within the organisation. The chaplain, so commissioned, has been endorsed and deployed by a higher authority. Unofficial Chaplains understand that they have been divinely commissioned for ministry outside the church, even though there will probably be no official recognition.

Joelle Kambamba, author of *The Chaplaincy Phenomena*, describes her foray into school chaplaincy as, "my response to God's call".[7] She felt personally commissioned by God for this ministry. The Bible records many occasions of commissioning. In the Old Testament, prophets, priests and kings were set apart for special service (1 Samuel 3; 16:1-13). In the New Testament, apostles

> Naval Chaplaincy has been christened 'the Silent Service', an epithet borrowed from the submarine branch. The point being that chaplaincy work often goes on unseen.

and missionaries were endorsed and deployed by way of ceremonies of spiritual significance (Acts 1:1-8; 13:1-3). These commissioning ceremonies were usually brief. What followed was more important—these people were *engaged in active service* in accordance with their divine deployment. They understood that their special ministry had been endorsed by the highest authority.

As an Unofficial Chaplain, your active service will *commence* and *continue* based on your *conviction* that it has been specially *commissioned* by God. That sense of spiritual commissioning is what matters most.

The Apostle Peter understood that *all* Christians are called and commissioned for ministry. He wrote of everyday Christians as "God's elect … who have been chosen … to be obedient to Jesus Christ" (1 Peter 1:1-2). He asserted that these ordinary believers were to prepare their minds for action (1 Peter 1:13). They had received a divine decree to do good, and to seek peace and pursue it (1 Peter 3:11). In their hearts, they were to pledge allegiance to Jesus as Lord and to always be prepared to share their Christian hope with others appropriately (1 Peter 3:15-16). These directives described some of the duties associated with their deployment *outside the church*. They were each commissioned for this kind of service to the people around them.

The Apostle's teaching still applies to *every* follower of Jesus. We are *all* commissioned for ongoing, everyday service to the people around us. This spiritual conviction doesn't require a special ceremony. Your chaplaincy ministry will be 'unofficial'. You won't have a title. But that doesn't matter. Divinely commissioned chaplains don't mind that their service is often unseen and unnoticed. Given the personal, and sometimes confidential, nature of the work it's to be expected. In fact, one naval chaplain christened the Chaplaincy Branch of the Royal Australian Navy 'the Silent

Service'. This is the affectionate nickname for the submarine branch.[8] The point is that naval chaplaincy work often goes on quietly 'below the surface'.

Actually, it's *because* a lot of unofficial chaplaincy work goes on unheralded and even under-appreciated that your sense of divine commissioning is so important. Your conviction regarding your calling *sustains* you. Chaplaincy work can feel lonely at times. It's heart work and, consequently, it can sometimes be hurtful. It can be hard work. It takes a lot of spiritual energy to serve Christ and others in a spirit of humble service.

Nevertheless, you *are* ordained for chaplaincy-type service. You *have* been endorsed and deployed by a higher authority. God has called you to be an Unofficial Chaplain to the people around you. And the good news is that your Father, who sees what is done in secret, will reward you (Matthew 6:4)! This first chapter concerns your commissioning because everything will flow out of that. Knowing this fortifies your faith for the mission!

So, are you willing to embrace your calling today? Are you willing to serve the people around you right now? Remember, you have been strategically placed where you are for special service *outside the church*. You have been purposely positioned in order to serve the people God has placed around you. Remind yourself of this divine deployment. Embrace your role as an Unofficial Chaplain! *The Unofficial Chaplain's Prayer* begins this way: *Today, I am commissioned to do good to the people around me.* Your actions will flow out of this conviction.

Having received your commission, the ongoing challenge is to fulfil your calling with skill and passion. As Colonel Brewer told his chaplains, "It is fundamentally important that a chaplain clearly understands his role within the unit and that he strives to fulfil that role competently and with conviction".[9]

The following chapters of this handbook will describe the role and responsibilities of a chaplain. These 'chaplaincy essentials' embrace:

a) a holistic ministry approach;
b) an ambassadorial function;
c) a preparedness to share the hope you have in Christ;
d) a willingness to leverage relationships for good;
e) the reality that antagonism is the inevitable reaction of some;
f) intercession as absolutely vital to the mission;
g) a lifestyle of nudging people in God's direction.

These challenges are great. Nevertheless, when chaplains apply themselves each day, and seek to incrementally develop their competency, then their capacity and capabilities gradually increase. There is great reward in embracing your commissioning as an eager student and a willing servant. So, seek to explore and answer questions like these:

- What ministry skills and expertise do I need to develop in order to be a better Unofficial Chaplain, and how can I best do that?
- How can I stay motivated in this divine deployment?

Today, commit yourself to the role that God has commissioned for you. Be an Unofficial Chaplain to the people around you.

2

HOLISTIC MINISTRY

Chaplains care for the whole person. Their spiritual ministry encompasses the whole of life. If there is any need that can be practically met–be it physical, emotional, relational, spiritual–a chaplain will endeavour, with God's help, to meet it. Chaplaincy ministry is holistic in nature. This is reflected in the compassionate actions of Jesus who fed the hungry, freed the oppressed, healed the sick, offered hope to people in trouble and comforted those who were grieving. Jesus readily did these things knowing that many of those He helped would not follow Him. Chaplains follow Christ's example by offering help to all.

The holistic nature of spiritual ministry has a culinary connection. Monks made minestrone. *Minestrone* is an Italian word derived from the Latin *ministrare*. The English words *minister* and *ministry* are sourced from there. At the heart of these words is the notion of simple service. All kinds of service. Minestrone soups were prepared by monks and kept warm on fires, always ready to be served up to weary travellers.

The parable of the Good Samaritan informs the ministry of a Good Chaplain.

This was a pressing physical need. Their primary response was a practical one. They made nourishing soup. Their spiritual service encompassed care for the whole person, whatever the need might have been. When they saw a need they could meet, they met it.

As an Unofficial Chaplain, your ministry is to the whole person. You are charged to "do good", whatever form that may take (1 Peter 3:11). As God enables you to see a need that *can* be met, so He will give you assistance in meeting it. Perhaps you can anticipate some of the needs that the people around you will have, sooner or later. It might be someone to talk to, a meal, a visit in hospital or a message of encouragement. There are so many simple ways to make a big difference. You need to be prepared to offer all kinds of support. Like those monks, you might have something helpful ready for when the need inevitably arises.

Chaplains provide holistic care without discrimination. They love the people around them, regardless of race, gender, orientation, religious or non-religious convictions and social status. As a chaplain, I have offered basic pastoral care to a Muslim, a bi-sexual person, atheists and many lapsed Roman Catholics. I don't need to approve of a person's lifestyle choices in order to care for them. The parable of the Good Samaritan informs the ministry of a Good Chaplain (Luke 10:25-37). As an Unofficial Chaplain, your charge is to do your best to alleviate suffering wherever it confronts you, whoever might be affected. Your simple acts of kindness, friendship and mercy should be freely rendered without prejudice.

From early times, chaplains were also advisers. They would help people, as best they could, make sense of life. They would also encourage good decision-making. While chaplains did not possess all wisdom, they had this advantage: they thought deeply about God and life. Consequently, they often had insights that were helpful to those unprepared for life's tragedies and spiritual possibilities. The primary source of their wisdom was the Bible.

Scripture has a great deal to say about life in this world. Its content is "God-breathed and is useful for teaching, rebuking, correcting and training in righteousness" (2 Timothy 3:16). It says, for example, "Whoever would love life and see good days must ... turn from evil and do good; they must seek peace and pursue it" (1 Peter 3:10-11). This is good and godly advice.

As an Unofficial Chaplain, you will need to know with increasing depth and insight what the Bible reveals about the whole of life. This is because a chaplain should encourage people to live a good life on God's terms. But don't bash them with the Bible. Share God's wisdom with gentleness and respect. There's an old saying that goes, "People don't care how much you know until they know how much you care." It still applies!

Chaplains are acutely aware of ultimate spiritual realities and eternal destinies. For this reason, chaplains desire to share the gospel of Jesus Christ with the people around them. This is fundamental in chaplaincy ministry. It is temporarily helpful to care for a person's physical wellbeing. It is good to provide all kinds of support. Nevertheless, it is ultimately disastrous if they end up losing their soul (Matthew 16:26). Our desire is to see people saved by grace through faith (Ephesians 2:8). Only God can ultimately save the whole person—soul *and* body (1 Cor. 15:42-44). For this reason, chaplains should seek opportunities to share God and His gospel with the people around them (Romans 1:16).

This holistic ministry is empowered by the Holy Spirit. The Holy Spirit ministers to the whole of life. The Bible declares that "God anointed Jesus of Nazareth with the Holy Spirit and power" and summarises the effects of the Holy Spirit's influence with the phrase, "He went around doing good"

(Acts 10:38). So, in the exercise of your unofficial chaplaincy ministry let the holistic good that you do be wholly empowered by the Holy Spirit.

Ask God, today, to help you see a need and meet it through the power of the Holy Spirit. Look for opportunities to:
- provide physical support
- offer emotional comfort
- help people find freedom
- bring healing
- give spiritual guidance
- serve without prejudice.

Chaplaincy ministry is holistic in nature. It is also supernatural in nature because we "do good" through the power of the Holy Spirit. Today, pray to God asking: *If someone has a need I can meet, enable me see it and meet it.*

3

AMBASSADOR FOR CHRIST

Tim Mander is a former CEO of Scripture Union and oversaw the early, massive growth of the nationally acclaimed school chaplaincy program.[10] He said of school chaplains, "These men and women of God are Christ's ambassadors on the frontline of ministry."[11] When you exercise your calling as an Unofficial Chaplain, the same can be said of you. You've left the safety of the church walls to serve on the frontline as an ambassador of Christ.

Chaplains represent God to the people around them. Their role is an ambassadorial one; their life and ministry should point people towards Christ (2 Corinthians 5:20). People expect this of chaplains. They do not expect them to be absolutely faultless but they *do* expect them to be consistently faithful. Chaplains are sometimes the only committed Christians who people know. So, as an Unofficial Chaplain, you need to be "wise in the way you act toward outsiders" and "make the most of every opportunity" (Colossians 4:5).

As an Unofficial Chaplain, your lifestyle should be consciously connected to your commissioning. Whatever you do, you should do it well. If your unofficial chaplaincy is exercised in the workplace, you should work "with all your heart, as working for the Lord" (Colossians 3:23). You need to be a whole-hearted contributor to the people and organisation that you serve. Your life should exemplify integrity, diligence, and forge a good reputation (1 Timothy 3:7).

As Colonel Brewer told his chaplains, "An Army chaplain is first and foremost an example, not only to those personnel of his faith, but to all … He will be watched carefully."[12] You need to be mindful of your spiritual influence. Your presence needs to have a positive impact on the people and the culture around you. This will go a long way towards creating the right conditions for spiritual conversations.

> In a sense, a chaplain's life should be prophetic in that it points people upward to Christ, to the kingdom of God, and to a new and abundant lifestyle.

Chaplains aim to imitate Christ and live lives worthy of imitation (1 Thessalonians 1:6). This is no easy calling given the complexity of the challenges around us. Hospital chaplain Kenneth Mitchell, by way of example, described an internist who was a notorious teller of dirty jokes and "loved to stop in my office to see if he could shock me with a new one."[13] Come what may, our charge is to somehow respond as we believe Jesus would. This ability to discern what Jesus would do flows from a deep commitment to His Lordship in your life. The Bible says, "in your hearts revere Christ as Lord" (1 Peter 3:15). Here, "the sense of fear or reverence for the Lord rather than the fear of men is reinforced."[14] The implication is a "constant willingness to speak up for Him, to confess one's allegiance to Him, and to witness fearlessly to His saving grace."[15]

This set-apartness means that a chaplain's life will probably stand out from the crowd. Our ambassadorship takes precedence over peer acceptance. Sadly, Colonel Brewer had come across chaplains "who strove so hard for acceptance that they became the hardest drinkers and cursers in the unit."[16] This indictment lists a tiny sample of the kinds of compromises that drag the gospel into disrepute and our chaplaincy to disdain. Better the example of a World War I chaplain, William McKenzie, who reportedly encouraged those he influenced to keep their consciences, "void of offence towards God and towards man."[17] "In a sense, a chaplain's life should be prophetic in that it points people upward to Christ, to the kingdom of God, and to a new and abundant lifestyle.

Of course, you will not be perfect. Chaplains get it wrong. Nevertheless, even when you sin or misrepresent Christ, *the way you repent and respond* in the aftermath of your sins and mistakes can bear witness to God's goodness and grace. The power of your apology or request for forgiveness will demonstrate the humble power of the Christian message. Your response when you have been offended or let down will afford another opportunity to give God glory. When you forgive, you are representing Christ who forgives. Jesus taught us to pray, "Forgive us our sins, for we also forgive everyone who sins against us" (Luke 11:4). In the exercise of your unofficial chaplaincy, there will be many occasions to unleash the power of forgiveness.

This ambassadorial calling involves sacrifice and a willingness to serve. Chaplains know this and enlist just the same. For me, this has meant filling countless water bottles for players and doing menial, pack-up-clean-up tasks behind the scenes, just as Jesus did (John 13:1-16). It has meant listening to people's problems and questions after-hours and responding out of love and concern (John 3:1-21). It has meant taking action when I've received late-night calls in times of crisis, and offering timely care in Jesus' name.

These kinds of sacrifices are endemic in chaplaincy ministry. Chaplaincy, at its best, imitates the selflessness of Jesus. Through service like this, we represent Him to those who have never read a Bible or connected with a church.

Today, accept your ambassadorial ministry and resolve, with God's help, to:

- imitate Christ and live a life worthy of imitation
- serve with all your heart
- not conform to the sinful behaviour of the people around us
- ask for and offer forgiveness
- be humble and commit to selfless service.

Ask God to help you be *a credible ambassador for Christ, one who serves diligently and models integrity.*

4

PREPARED TO SHARE HOPE

Many of the people around us are living without real, substantial hope. For an elite sportsperson, for example, the horizon of hope can be the next game or the next season. Chaplains offer the lasting hope of life with Jesus Christ. As the National Director of Sports Chaplaincy Australia, Cameron Butler, wrote in the Foreword of *Our Daily Bread—Sports Chaplaincy Edition*, "We desperately need hope and … hope is sure for anyone when they are in a personal relationship with Jesus Christ."[18] Unofficial Chaplains must be prepared to share that hope.

Preparation requires forethought. You have made yourself ready. You're prepared to pass the test. You know how you will respond and you believe that God will help you do that well. Your ambassadorial lifestyle has raised people's curiosity and, sometimes, their consternation. This is because your life is different in a good way.

People will want to know the reasons why. They are intrigued. As the Bible says, you need to always "be prepared to give an answer to everyone who asks you to give the reason for the hope that you have" (1 Peter 3:15). As an Unofficial Chaplain, you will have prepared appropriate answers to anticipated questions. When the time is right, your words

> Be prepared to tell the whole gospel story and to defend the faith without getting defensive.

need to point people upward to God.

While the Bible predicts that Christians will face interrogation at formal trials on account of their faith, there is also an expectation that they will frequently be asked questions in informal, spontaneous and ordinary conversations.[19] With this in mind, the Apostle Peter instructed ordinary Christians to be ready for the enquiries when they inevitably came. This expectation mandated preparation. They needed to be prepared to share hope!

As an Unofficial Chaplain, you should expect questions about faith to be raised in ordinary conversations and perhaps even a little interrogation sometimes. When people are comfortable around you, these conversations become as natural as talking about the footy or your family. Your answers should sensitively declare your gospel-hope concerning the future. "Christians are, in other words, expected to be prepared to speak at any moment about God's salvation of His people through Jesus Christ and how this salvation manifests itself at the end of history."[20] In other words, be prepared to tell the whole gospel story and to defend the faith without getting defensive. These spiritual conversations will usually build over time, so don't feel unnecessary pressure to tell the whole gospel message every time. As the Apostle Paul said to King Agrippa: "Short time or long - I pray to God that not only you but all who are listening to me today may become what I am ... " (Acts 26:29).

So, how can you be ready to share your faith? You can make a start by:

- learning to share your own salvation story. What better way to share than by simply telling enquirers what Jesus has done in your life?
- researching and sharing the best gospel presentations available in print and on-line.

In sharing your faith, be sure to emphasise the reason that you have *hope* (1 Peter 3:15). People are desperate for hope. And, our sure hope is in the Person and Work of Christ. Make sure they hear that!

The people around you will also have questions and reservations about the Christian faith. How can you be better prepared to defend the faith? Recent Australian research reveals there are nine common obstacles that people have to accepting the Christian faith.[21] They are problems related to suffering, the Bible, the supernatural, religious violence, exclusive faith, church abuse, science and God, homosexuality and the church. You need to formulate some Biblical and personal answers to these wide-spread concerns and/or point people to reliable resources that will help alleviate their concerns. There are many excellent apologetics resources available. Become familiar with the best of these and share them around. You don't have to be a theological expert on every topic.

You must be prepared to respond in the right way. It is very easy to get defensive, aggressive or dismissive when sharing or upholding the Christian faith. This is especially true when objections are framed in belligerent or condescending ways. Therefore, chaplains should be open-hearted and relationally generous when answering faith-questions or objections.

The Bible says, "Let your conversation be always full of grace, seasoned with salt, so that you may know how to answer everyone" (Colossians 4:6), and, "do this [give an answer] with gentleness and respect, keeping a clear conscience, so that those who speak maliciously against your good behaviour in Christ may be ashamed of their slander" (1 Peter 3:15-16). The manner in which you give your answer often determines the receptiveness of the enquirer. As an Unofficial Chaplain, you will ideally maintain healthy relationships with the people around you. To this end, the tone of your answers should seek to preserve respect, encourage exploration and strengthen rapport.

Unofficial Chaplains are always prepared to share their faith and answer questions in ways that encourage receptivity. Today:

- get ready for faith questions to come up in conversation
- be prepared to share about your personal spiritual journey
- be inquisitive and find out the big questions that people are asking
- provide reasonable answers to those questions or point enquirers in the right direction
- make sure that the manner in which you answer questions encourages friendship and dialogue.

Reflect on this line from *The Unofficial Chaplain's Prayer*:

May I always be prepared to share my faith and hope in simple, appropriate ways.

5

LEVERAGE RELATIONSHIPS FOR GOOD

Chaplaincy is a ministry of connectivity. Chaplaincy is a ministry of proximity. The success of chaplaincy rests on the strength and closeness of relationships. Extensive interviews with Australian Sports Chaplains, "suggested that in order for opportunities to present themselves the chaplains first had to build rapport and develop their role so that they were fully accepted by players, families and other people around the club."[22]

This is especially true for an Unofficial Chaplain. While a military chaplain may be able to pull rank, an Unofficial Chaplain has no such authority. You can serve but you cannot summon. You can invite but you cannot insist.

Yet, this is the adventure of chaplaincy. You relate with the people around you not knowing when God will break in, not knowing when their lives will open to you. You are waiting and hoping, but not from above. You are on the front line and down in the trenches with the people you

> As every chaplain knows, there is an undeniable correlation between people's acceptance of you and their openness to your ministry.

serve. To quote Colonel Brewer again: "Respect must be earned and nurtured carefully ... A chaplain must participate and be involved in as many unit activities as possible ... His commitment and sharing of demanding activities will do more for his acceptance as a worthy team member than most other endeavours combined."[23]

As every chaplain knows, there is an undeniable correlation between people's acceptance of *you* and their openness to *your ministry*. The greater the level of trust and acceptance, the greater the potential for truth and influence. This relational leverage can be used for good and godly purposes. There are three identifiable levels of influence in the exercise of unofficial chaplaincy ministry. They are outlined below.

<u>First level</u>

First, people need to become confident that you are a decent, trustworthy human being. They need to get to know you and feel comfortable around you. People will evaluate you. They might discover that you are a Christian. This all takes time. It certainly helps if they end up liking you. Earning basic trust at this early stage is foundational for the ministry of unofficial chaplaincy. Your usual interactions ought to inspire confidence and earn you a good reputation. This happens when you simply:

- serve people in small ways
- meet or exceed expectations
- talk about common, constructive things
- avoid destructive conversations
- have fun on social occasions
- participate positively.

All this happens in the normal course of everyday life. At this elementary level, you will be asking God for increasing favour in your relationships with the people around you. So, get involved in your workplace or team's Social Club if they have one. Participate in the kinds of events that will help people get to know you on a friendly, casual basis.

Second level

Relationships deepen when you connect with people outside of the usual, everyday context. When you spend time with people 'after-hours', friendships reach a new level. We will call them 'second level' relationships. You might catch up for a cup of coffee, invite them over to your house for a meal or out for a game of golf. It could be anything. As an Unofficial Chaplain, you need to do this intentionally and appropriately. This relational bridge-building encourages genuine friendship and increases the likelihood of openness to talk about deeper things, including spirituality. It will also open doors for ministry during times of crisis. So meet with people away from your usual context. Spend extraordinary time with the people around you. These second-level relationships are more meaningful. Plan to catch up with someone soon. Ask God:

- which of your friendships are experiencing His favour in direct response to your prayer?
- what would be the best way to encourage deepening connections?
- to help you invest quality time in order to build meaningful relationships.

Third level

Some relationships will turn into spiritual friendships. We will call them 'third level' relationships. As an Unofficial Chaplain, you will now guide these people toward faith in Christ. Your 'multi-level' friendship will ensure that they have a familiar face in this unfamiliar, spiritual territory. During this exciting stage, you need to be ready to answer all the questions you can, as well as share what you have learned along the way. It is also the right time to introduce your friends to a wider circle of Christians and to your local church. Nevertheless, you will still need to be there for them. After all, chaplaincy is a ministry of proximity. Ask God:

- who He is preparing to accept Christ?
- what you need to do in order to be an excellent spiritual friend?
- to reveal the right time to connect your friend to a wider circle of Christians.

Unofficial Chaplains do all they can to encourage acceptance and openness in everyday relationships. This basic connectivity increases likelihood of deepening, more meaningful camaraderie. This relational leverage requires an extraordinary investment of time. The prayerful goal is that some of these relationships will become spiritual friendships as the people we serve come to know Christ as Saviour. As you pray *The Unofficial Chaplain's Prayer*, you will be asking God to help *your relationships deepen and your spiritual influence increase as you invest time in people*.

A Chaplaincy Story

Aaron* came to the Footy Club as an 18 year old. I used to fill his water bottle at training and we'd have short talks. He was homesick, so after a while I invited him over for a meal with my family. Over time we got to know each other more. Aaron had a church background and, because he showed interest, we started meeting to study the Bible together when his training and travel schedule allowed. It became a 'third level' relationship. Some months later, he committed his life to Christ. It was my privilege to help him learn how to pray and to connect him with a local church. He has since been signed with another Club and moved on. I still think of him regularly and continue to pray for him.

* Not the player's real name.

6

ANTICIPATE ANTAGONISM

The Bible says, "If it is possible, as far as it depends on you, live at peace with everyone" (Romans 12:18). A chaplain is a person of peace. Sometimes, during periods of extreme conflict, chaplains have shouldered arms. Many have exhibited great courage under fire. These grave and exceptional times notwithstanding, chaplains generally have heeded the Bible's call to "seek peace and pursue it" (1 Peter 3:11). More often than not, chaplains have displayed true meekness—that is, the Christ-like trait of not retaliating when it was within their power to exact revenge (1 Peter 2:21-23). This was the example that Jesus left for those enlisted in His service.

The work of a chaplain is not always appreciated or welcomed. Not everyone is open to receive care from a chaplain-type person. Some people have a strictly secular view of life. Others have a strong commitment to a different religion. Your unofficial chaplaincy might therefore be considered

> You should expect some level of opposition to your unofficial chaplaincy role and resolve to conduct yourself in a manner worthy of your high calling.

an unwelcome intrusion or your faith a delusion. Some chaplains have experienced considerable rejection. A World War I chaplain wrote of being barely tolerated and given the "cold shoulder."[24] The challenge then was to "maintain a cheerful and gracious attitude, together with a deep spirituality."[25] So you should expect some level of opposition to your unofficial chaplaincy role and resolve to conduct yourself in a manner worthy of your high calling.

The Bible anticipates that we will sometimes suffer for doing good (1 Peter 3:14). Rather than abandoning your calling, you need to accept rejection as the reaction of some to your good behaviour in Christ. You also need to develop disciplined ways to respond. Here are some ways to respond to the rejection:

1) Seek peace and pursue it (1 Peter 3:11). This requires creative exploration of possible solutions. This requires constant exertion of spiritual strength. In this fallen world, peace is not routine. It is a sad fact that dissension is often the default setting. Some people like it that way. A large part of chaplaincy ministry involves attempts at restoring broken relationships and encouraging harmony among the people around us. Jesus said, "Blessed are the peacemakers" (Matthew 5:9). Chaplains need to model peacemaking. When you do not retaliate in the face of antagonism, you model the way of peace.

2) Love your enemies and do good to those who hate you (Luke 6:27). This command from Jesus requires more than displaying restraint. It demands that we actively bless those who reject us. Do not antagonise those who oppose your ministry. Find ways to add value to their lives.

3) Love your enemies and pray for those who persecute you (Matthew 5:44). Jesus prayed for those who crucified Him asking, "Father, forgive them" (Luke

23:34). He blessed those who cursed Him. In the course of your deployment, the same will be required of you. Pray strenuously for the people who resent your unofficial chaplaincy ministry.

4) Entrust yourself and the circumstances "to Him who judges justly" (1 Peter 2:23). Christ did not retaliate. He did not even raise His voice in His own defence. His life was lived openly before friend and foe. People could evaluate the evidence. Let your good reputation speak for itself and give God room to respond as He sees fit, and, let your conduct be such "that those who speak maliciously against your good behaviour in Christ may be ashamed of their slander" (1 Peter 3:16).

1 Peter 3:14 says, "Do not fear their threats; do not be frightened." It is fear that keeps most people from sharing Christ with the people around them—fear that we won't have all the answers; fear of rejection; fear of hostility; fear that our open faith might jeopardise future prospects of advancement. We need to meet fear with faith. Anticipating antagonism, reconciling with its inevitability, and finding courage in God are keys to effective chaplaincy ministry.

When we are convinced that God has *commissioned* us, when people know that we *care* for them, when we embrace our *ambassadorial* role, when we're *prepared* to share our hope, when we invest in genuine *relationships*, when we *intercede* for friends and enemies, then our faith is fortified.

It's also important to keep in mind that your biggest persecutors can become your best promoters. The Apostle Paul's story was just like that (Galatians 1:13). Not everyone at the footy clubs I've served in has been positive about my chaplaincy presence. Quite a few people have given me the 'cold shoulder'. Then, after a player tragically suicided, I was heavily involved in team and staff welfare.

It was then that a high profile player commented, "I used to wonder why the #@%* we had a chaplain. Now I think I know." Opinions can change, so hope and pray for the best! Keep believing for a breakthrough moment in the lives of those who are antagonistic towards you.

Today, prepare yourself for some opposition. Do your best to respond to rejection in a disarming manner. Make every effort to live peacefully and positively with the people whom you are called to serve. Pray sincerely the portion of *The Unofficial Chaplain's Prayer* that asks: *Give me the strength to accept antagonism and to respond with a blessing.*

7

INTERCESSORY PRAYER

Chaplains should be people who pray. They should intercede on behalf of the people who they serve. In the Bible, intercession is the form of prayer on behalf of another with a view to obtaining help for that other.[26] This is a major duty of chaplaincy ministry, and we should pray in faith believing that "the eyes of the Lord are on the righteous and His ears are attentive to their prayer" (1 Peter 3:12). And, we do much of our praying 'outside the church'. As one hospital chaplain put it, a chaplain's prayers are "seldom uttered in the quiet of a church, but more often on the run, or down the hall, or as he hangs up the phone."[27] Oswald Chambers was a chaplain who died while serving in World War I. He wrote, "We tend to use prayer as a last resort, but God wants it to be our first line of defence. We pray when there is nothing else we can do, but God wants us to pray before we do anything at all." Prayer is vital! There is a correlation between prayer power and effectiveness in chaplaincy ministry.

Pray *for* the people around you as part of your personal

> When an Unofficial Chaplain prays aloud with someone experiencing trauma, God is openly invited into the situation.

prayer life. Pray for them by name. Bring to God their problems and aspirations. The deeper the relationship that you have, the more informed your prayers will be.

Ask God to open the door of their hearts to Jesus Christ.

Pray against the diabolical plans of their spiritual enemies.

Pray for those who oppose you in your unofficial chaplaincy ministry.

Pray for God's protection and blessing upon those things that you do together—be it work, study or play.

Ask the Holy Spirit to prompt your prayers and help fortify your faith. The Spirit of God helps us in our prayer life and intercedes for us (Romans 8:27). I have an extensive list of names in a prominent place on the wall of my study. It's my Prayer Wall!

I make short notes as I recall snippets of important conversations that I've had with the people on that list. I intercede for them and ask them follow-up questions from time to time. It's amazing the positive feedback you get when people realize you have remembered what's going on for them.

Pray *with* the people you serve when appropriate opportunities arise. When there is a crisis, be prepared to pray aloud with people. Look for opportunities to pray with people when they share with you their deep concerns. Make the prayer short, simple and sincere. As a chaplain I have prayed in front of thirty hardened sportsmen when news of a tragedy broke. No one resisted it. Many were helped by it and thanked me for it.

When the right moment presents itself, simply ask if it would be OK for you to pray, there and then, with and for those concerned. Perhaps your offer will be rejected. This is rare. Better that you asked. People who know and trust you will usually respond positively. When an Unofficial Chaplain prays aloud with someone experiencing trauma, God is openly invited into the situation. Who knows what God will do as we pray openly in Jesus' name? Give God both the opportunity and the glory. In this way, you will exemplify a prayerful, God-oriented life. People need to see that.

Teach people to pray. As an Unofficial Chaplain, your role is not only to be a Christian person serving in your context; you should also encourage spiritual development in others. This is especially important in 'third level' relationships when you function as a spiritual friend and coach. Jesus' disciples asked if He could teach them to pray (Luke 11:1). While Jesus passionately interceded for them (John 17:6-19), He also encouraged them in their own prayer life. He gave them a model-prayer to help them start. We call it 'The Lord's Prayer'. Think about ways to help people start their own conversations with God.

It was so powerful to hear 'Aaron' (*mentioned at the end of Chapter 5*) praying for the first time. It was a hesitant, mumbled prayer for sure, but a real breakthrough for him! He started to pray regularly at home and more confidently when we met. To my great surprise, he even turned up to a church prayer meeting! I'll never forget him praying aloud in a circle of people that night. I was so amazed and pleased and felt that God was smiling on the whole situation.

Pray with *other Christians*. Are there other Christians in your workplace or on your team? Are they willing to meet with you to pray for the unsaved people around you? There is so much power in praying together! Here's a great chaplaincy story from a large, mineral-processing plant. The Unofficial Chaplain reported:

> I overheard some blokes talking about these 'churchies' that meet every Friday during their lunch breaks—down the back end of the plant—to pray for the company. As far as these blokes were concerned it was, "Good on them. It can't hurt. We need all the

help we can get." With around 700 people working here, word's getting round and it's made some good conversation. Praise the Lord!

Even non-Christians can be positive about intercession!

Today, as you enter into service as an Unofficial Chaplain, begin with prayer. Set the scene spiritually. Pray for the people around you by name.

Take this opportunity to pray *The Unofficial Chaplain's Prayer*, particularly the line: *Stir me, Holy Spirit, to pray for people privately and with them opportunely.*

Chaplain Oswald Chambers wrote: "Jesus Christ carries on intercession for us in heaven; the Holy Ghost carries on intercession in us on earth; and we the saints have to carry on intercession for all men."

I totally agree!

8

NUDGE

The dictionary describes a *nudge* as a gentle push, especially with the elbow, to get someone's attention.[28] Chaplaincy ministry is more about nudging than Bible bashing. The Bible encourages us to share our faith "with gentleness and respect, keeping a clear conscience" (1 Peter 3:15-16). A chaplain recognises that there are often many incremental steps in a person's journey to Jesus. Our role is to gently and opportunely turn people's attention towards God and the gospel. There are a number of ways to nudge people along. Below are some of them.

1) Your own, ambassadorial example should get people's attention. The way you live should preach the gospel of Jesus Christ. As Australian soldiers allegedly said of Chaplain McKenzie, "He made religion live and lived it himself, never ramming it down tired men's throat[s]."[29] The living hope that we have is hard to hide.

> Chaplaincy is a ministry of proximity. So much of the ministry happens 'elbow to elbow' as people do things together.

Our godly attitudes and actions will cause people to look and listen.

2) Displaying courage under pressure gets people's attention. This is especially true when you are on the front line and elbow to elbow 'in the trenches'. In a World War I letter from the frontline, a chaplain wrote: "A thousand eyes are on the [chaplain], to see whether his bearing is as bold and fearless when Death is reaching out his bony hand... Should he shrink or fail in the test, then where, think you, will his influence be?"[30] Showing good courage elevates people's perception of you and the faith that you profess.

3) Humble service gets people's attention. The Christian faith is founded on sacrificial service. When you do the grimy, inconvenient jobs that no one else wants to do and look after the interests of others, you imitate Christ's loving humility and personify the grace of the gospel (Philippians 2:1-8).

4) Stir the conscience of the people around you. People intuitively know right from wrong and often choose what is wrong (Romans 2:14-15). Because many of their peers participate in the same sins, their consciences can become insensitive (1 Timothy 4:2). When you do the right thing you point people towards the truth and often convict their consciences. A chaplain might stand up for someone being bullied or speak the truth even when its unpopular. At our best, chaplains refuse to be involved in malicious gossip and demonstrate integrity in potentially compromising situations. Perhaps the Holy Spirit will use these occasions to help those around you to see their need for forgiveness and salvation (John 16:8). During my time as a Rugby League chaplain, there have been many occasions when people have come to me, publicly and privately, and apologised for inappropriate behaviour.

Chaplains can stir the consciences of the people we serve by demonstrating the kind of lifestyle that pleases God and treats people with dignity. Having a clear conscience yourself is, of course, very important when it comes to the integrity of your Christian witness.

5) Invite people to investigate the Christian faith for themselves. Meet with people who show genuine interest in spiritual things and study the Bible together. Some people are more willing to be nudged than others. World War I chaplain, Frederick Miles, wrote that "Every evening I have gathered my more spiritual men for Bible study and prayer."[31] Perhaps every evening will be a little too often. Just do not miss the opportunity to foster potential 'third level' relationships.

Chaplaincy is a ministry of proximity. So much of the ministry happens 'elbow to elbow' as people do things together. As an Unofficial Chaplain, you are best placed to give the people around you a gentle nudge towards Jesus.

And, work the 'Engels'.

James F. Engel developed a simple scale as a way of representing the sometimes long journey from knowing little or nothing about God through to Christian maturity.[32] The model illustrates the *process* of religious conversion that usually involves various decision-making steps along the way to becoming a Christian. It also demonstrates the accumulative value of little nudges in the right direction. Jesus, for example, plotted people on their journey in relation to God. He said of some, "You belong to your father, the devil" (John 8:44). They couldn't have been further away! He said to a spiritual seeker, "You are not far from the kingdom of God" (Mark 12:34). And to Zacchaeus, "Today salvation has come to this house" (Luke 19:9).

Sure, we don't always know exactly where a person is on their God-journey. Jesus cautioned us that sometimes it's hard to tell (Matthew 13:24-30). Nevertheless, it can be helpful to 'plot' someone on the Engel scale to assist in your consideration of what their next step might be. And, it's when you have genuine, deepening friendships with people that you can best judge the nudge that's needed.

Today, point the people around you towards Jesus.

Make sure your life makes Christianity attractive.

Show spiritual courage under pressure.

Do the menial tasks that help people without any fuss.

Do the right thing—it will encourage others to do the same.

Determine if there is someone you could invite to explore the Christian faith further, and pray sincerely *The Unofficial Chaplain's Prayer* that asks: *Lord, help me nudge someone in your direction.*

9

FLOODING THE ZONE

God has strategically located His people in workplaces, neighbourhoods, community groups, educational institutions and on sports teams. In AFL and NFL there's a strategy called 'flooding the zone'. This is a tactical deployment of numerous players into vital areas for offensive or defensive purposes. It's a tactic that's employed as part of a winning strategy.

God is 'flooding the zone'. From heaven's perspective, there's a lot of spiritual coverage across communities and across this nation. It's being rolled out in country towns and sprawling cities. While God's people normally gather regularly to worship Him—often on Sundays and often in buildings— we are mostly scattered all over the place, right through the week. We are sent into the world and onto the front line. This is God's good purpose. The objective of the 'flooding' is the spiritual saturation of the nation. It's part of God's plan to win the nation!

We are all surrounded by people whom God loves and longs to bring into his spiritual family. Our job—alongside being a great worker, leader, team-member, contributor, citizen and such—is to reach the people around us. You are there to help the people around you succeed in every way, including spiritually. You are there to help point people towards Jesus.

Like the unnamed, everyday people mentioned in Acts 11:20, our contact with people should, sooner or later, include sharing the good news about the Lord Jesus. These Christians 'flooded the zone' in Antioch and the Lord's hand was with them to great effect!

You are commissioned for this same purpose, with this same hope. The people around you will be blessed as you care for them holistically, as an ambassador for Christ. Your preparedness to share your hope will elevate some relationships into genuine spiritual friendships. Sure, there will be some opposition. You're ready for that. But as you pray and nudge people towards Jesus, God will use you for His glory.

And, you won't be alone! You are part of a network of thousands of people that God has deployed across our nation to reach people. We all share the calling to special ministry *outside the church*. God is deploying unofficial-chaplain-type people everywhere, in order to connect the world with His love and salvation. I believe that God has purposed to reach our nation through the collective effort of His people who are intentionally 'flooding the zone' in every community.

For those of us who don't identify as 'evangelists' or 'preachers', there is an authentic and effective alternative. We can be knowingly and willingly deployed as 'Unofficial Chaplains' in workplaces, on university campuses, on sports team, *wherever*. Your role in God's plan is vital! You are, in certain contexts, a natural 'insider'. Consequently and strategically, when it's all said and done, there's no one better positioned to reach the people around you than *you*!

God's people are on the move. God's church is moving beyond the church walls and onto the front lines. God's church is being mobilised to flood every zone in every community. And, *you* are called to be a part of an 'open-the-flood-gates' movement that is poised to saturate this nation as we positively nudge people toward Jesus! You are commissioned for this mission as an 'Unofficial Chaplain'.

POSTSCRIPT

"A good chaplain is a priceless asset, and the spiritual reward from doing a job well done must be profound."[33] That's how Colonel Brewer concluded his talk to army chaplains. *You* have been commissioned to function as an Unofficial Chaplain, a calling to everyday service to the people around you.

Your challenge is to be fully engaged in this ministry; to be there *with* people; to be there *for* people; to 'do good' as an ambassador for Christ. You have been strategically positioned for this purpose.

Some people will be open to your ministry. Some people will reject it. Some people will not appreciate it until they experience your help in a time of crisis. In my own sports-chaplaincy ministry, it took a crisis for some to see the value of my service. Someone committed suicide. I was asked to be there to support those who were grieving. It was during this time that an influential player said, "I used to wonder why … we had a chaplain. Now I think I know." If you persist in your ministry, there will be moments when people will gain an appreciation for the role you play in their lives. After the memorial service for the player who passed away, a senior club official wrote me this email:

> *I cannot thank you enough for what you have done for our club and its players this week. Mate, your friendship, compassion, leadership and support were of the highest quality and something we will always treasure. On behalf of me and the players please accept our deepest thanks.*

God bless you, in your Unofficial Chaplaincy ministry!

ENDNOTES

1. Michael Gladwin ('Captains of the Soul', Big Sky Publishing Pty Ltd, Newport, Australia, 2013) p. 2.
2. Encyclopedia Britannica (2013); Chaplain; available: http://www.britannica.com/EBchecked/topic/106107/chaplain; retrieved: 19 August 2013.
3. E. A. Livingstone, 'chaplain' (Oxford Concise Dictionary of the Christian Church, Oxford University Press, New York, 2000) p. 110.
4. Michael Petras, 'Australian Baptists and the First World War in Retrospect', (Australian Baptists and World War I, ed. Michael Petras, Baptist Historical Society of NSW, 2009) p. 22-23.
5. Colonel C. J. Brewer, AM Chief of Staff 2nd Division; 'Opening Address – Chaplains Conference – Nov 93'.
6. Roy Williams ('Post God Nation', Harper Collins Publishers Australia, 2015) p. 283.
7. Joelle Kabamba, 'The Chaplaincy Phenomenon' (Spencer Publishing, Brisbane, Australia) p. 23.
8. Rowan Strong (Chaplains in the Royal Australian Navy, UNSW Press, Australia, 2012) p. vi.
9. Colonel C. J. Brewer, AM Chief of Staff 2nd Division; 'Opening Address – Chaplains Conference – Nov 93'.
10. http://www.timmander.com.au/index.php?web_page_name=abouttim
11. Foreword Tim Mander, Joelle Kabamba, 'The Chaplaincy Phenomenon' (Spencer Publishing, Brisbane, Australia) p. 8.
12. Colonel C. J. Brewer, AM Chief of Staff 2nd Division; 'Opening Address – Chaplains Conference – Nov 93'.
13. Kenneth R. Mitchell, 'Hospital Chaplain' (The Westminster Press, Philadelphia, 1972) p. 21.
14. Wayne Grudem, '1 Peter' (Tyndale New Testament Commentaries, Eerdmans, Grand Rapids, Michigan, 1998) p. 152.
15. Scot McKnight, '1 Peter' (The New Application Commentary, Zondervan, Grand Rapids, Michigan, 1996) p. 213.
16. Colonel C. J. Brewer, AM Chief of Staff 2nd Division; 'Opening Address – Chaplains Conference – Nov 93'.
17. Col Stringer, "Fighting' McKenzie: Anzac Chaplain' (Col Stringer Ministries, Robina, Australia, 2002) p. 41.
18. Cameron Butler, 'it matters' ('Our Daily Bread – Sports Chaplaincy Edition, RBC Ministries, Grand Rapids, Michigan, 2014) p. 3.
19. M. Stibbs and A. F. Walls, '1 Peter' (Tyndale New Testament Commentaries, Wm. B. Eerdmans Publishing Company, Grand Rapids, 1983) p. 135.
20. Scot McKnight, '1 Peter' (The New Application Commentary, Zondervan, Grand Rapids, Michigan, 1996) p. 214.
21. Karl Faase ('Towards Belief DVD and Discussion Guide', olivetreemedia, 2013)
22. Stephen Reid and Philip Hughes; Christian Research Association Research Paper No. 13, 'The Values and Benefits of Sports Chaplaincy in Australia', September 2013, p. 5.
23. Colonel C. J. Brewer, AM Chief of Staff 2nd Division; 'Opening Address – Chaplains Conference – Nov 93'.
24. 'Letters from the Front', (Australian Baptists and World War I, ed. Michael Petras, Baptist Historical Society of N.S.W., 2009) p. 78. Source: The Australian Baptist, May 22 1917, p. 1-2; Register of Education Committee of Baptist Union of NSW, 1902 – 27 (Baptist Historical Society of NSW Archives).
25. ibid
26. R. S. Wallace, 'Intercession' (The International Standard Bible Encyclopedia, Eerdmans, Grand Rapids, Michigan) Vol. 2, p. 858.
27. Kenneth R. Mitchell, 'Hospital Chaplain' (The Westminster Press, Philadelphia, 1972) p. 16.
28. Ed. G. A. Wilkes, 'nudge' (The Collins English Dictionary, Australian edition, William Collins Sons & Co. Ltd., Great Britain, 1990) p. 1055.
29. Col Stringer, "Fighting' McKenzie: Anzac Chaplain' (Col Stringer Ministries, Robina, Australia, 2002) p. 93.
30. 'Letters from the Front', (Australian Baptists and World War I, ed. Michael Petras, Baptist Historical Society of N.S.W., 2009) p. 78. Source: The Australian Baptist, May 22 1917, p. 1-2; Register of Education Committee of Baptist Union of NSW, 1902 – 27 (Baptist Historical Society of NSW Archives).
31. Michael Petras, 'Australian Baptists and the First World War in Retrospect', (Australian Baptists and World War I, ed. Michael Petras, Baptist Historical Society of NSW, 2009) p. 26.
32. James F. Engel and H. Wilbert Norton, 'What's Gone Wrong with the Harvest' (Zondervan, Grand Rapids, Michigan, 1976) p. 45.
33. Colonel C. J. Brewer, AM Chief of Staff 2nd Division; 'Opening Address – Chaplains Conference – Nov 93'.

WHAT OTHERS ARE SAYING ABOUT THIS BOOK …

This is a really helpful little book, written by an official chaplain about what it might look like if we all adopted the posture of an unofficial chaplain in the contexts where God has placed us. Pretty cool idea. Very practical and easy to read.

Michael Frost
Vice Principal Morling College Sydney, Director of the Tinsley Institute, Author Incarnate and The Road to Missional

Warren Crank nails the simplicity of unofficial chaplaincy—something he's personally discovered true-blue for our community as a sports chaplain. And it's for everyone with a genuine relationship with Jesus Christ. Aussies don't want religion but they do want authentic chaplains. Someone brave enough and close enough to care. I highly recommend you explore Warren's fresh perspective on informal chaplaincy. He challenges the way we relate to each other.

Rev. Cameron Butler
National Director Sports Chaplaincy Australia Inc.

The Unofficial Chaplain provides a cohesive and refreshing model for living an intentional and missional Christian life in an increasingly secular world. It is practical and inspirational. I recommend it and believe that God will use it to stimulate ministry and mission to people who are *outside the church*.

Stephen Gaukroger
Director Clarion Trust International, author and senior church leader in the UK having pastored two large churches and served as President of the Baptist Union of Great Britain

ABOUT THE AUTHOR

B. Min. (ACT); Grad. Dip. Min. (QBCM); Dip. Theol. (QBCM)
Warren Crank has been pastoring in Queensland for more than 20 years. He's been Lead Pastor of Ipswich Baptist Church and Northreach Baptist Church in Townsville. Recently, he has founded the Red Dirt Church Movement - a small collective of simple churches. Warren is currently a Regional Consultant for Queensland Baptists and leader of their Church Planting arm.

Warren has been Chaplain for the North Queensland Cowboys (NRL), the Norths Devils (QRL) and is currently Chaplain for the Brisbane Broncos (NRL).

Warren is also the author of **The Resolute Leader: A Handbook on Leadership Development**. He and his wife, Ellen, live in Brisbane and have three sons.